WALK DEEP

For Dee,

May your path
Surprise you with
beauty & magic.

Abigail

Walk
Deep

POEMS

Abigail Morgan Prout

WAYFARER BOOKS

BERKSHIRE MOUNTAINS, MASS.

WAYFARER BOOKS

WWW.WAYFARERBOOKS.ORG

Published in 2022 by Wayfarer Books
Cover Design and Interior Design by Leslie M. Browning
Cover Illustration by © Lisla
ISBN 978-1-956368-23-9
First Edition Trade Paperback

10 9 8 7 6 5 4 3 2 1

Look for our titles in paperback, ebook, and audiobook wherever books are sold.
Wholesale offerings for retailers available through Ingram.

Wayfarer Books is committed to ecological stewardship.
We greatly value the natural environment and invest in
environmental conservation. For each book purchased in our
online store we plant one tree.

*"In every walk with nature,
one receives far more than (s)he seeks."*
—JOHN MUIR

This book is dedicated to Lopez Hill
on Lopez Island, Washington. Every day I walk in
her generous woods, emerging with
the inspiration to share.

Also for our children, Nonie and Jax,
and to all of the children.

May you find yourselves in Nature.

CONTENTS

MOTHER TREE

THE GEMELS

HIDDEN MIRROR POND

GROTTO: RUSTLE OF SWORD FERNS

THE VIEW FROM THE HAMMOCK AT THE TOP OF THE WORLD

Boughs: They Reach but Cannot Touch

Ghost Root

Out of the Woods, Under the Sky

Down into Owl Valley

WALK

walk
walk deep
walk deep in
walk deep in the forest
walk deep in the forest for hours
walk deep in the forest for hours everyday
walk deep in the forest for hours
walk deep in the forest
walk deep in
walk deep
walk

ONE

Before there were sides
there was One
One pulse becoming
One rhythm drumming
One

And that One was pure
and great and round
in perfect echo
of unbroken sound
One

But no One witnessed
the glowing orb
no direction chosen
no learning absorbed
No One

So Creator
birthed the "other"
with the highest intention
of witness: a sister, a brother
Other

And so it began
from Self to selves
from Us to them
from We to me
the great forgetting of One began
No One remembered to remember
the One
No One

But so as evolution swings
calibration finds us
longing to sing
a song to guide ourselves back home
past sinew, muscle, hope and bone
Home

One pulse becoming
One rhythm drumming
Before there were sides
there was One
This One

Warriors of Light

In this struggle
there is no light
without dark

My willingness
to respond
with trust

Finding the place
inside that would die
for this cause

Shifts the water
in the river of
human tomorrows

If not for warriors
there would be
no freedom

BLUR OF GRACE

Everyone who is awake
through a private tangled wood
rides their own personal edge
at a break-necking speed

In a blur of grace, a deer arcs
surely another will follow
prisoners of their urges
just like you and me

One foot upon the brake,
one hand upon the throttle
these are wild driving times,
wild thriving, striving times

I will keep my lights on high
senses reaching, widening
alert to any lunging, lurching
up from shady bracken

We just cannot predict
what might next emerge
leaping from outside edges
much less stop to consider all the
universes exploding from within

A PATH WITH NO PATH

"Now it is time," declare Patience and Commitment, dressed in their matching denim coveralls, "to build beauty at the edge."

Creativity chimes in, bending slow to shy Intuition, so as not to startle. Talkative Collaboration interrupts, catching Beauty in the act.

All who listen are busy stacking rock on rock on rock on the banks of what is known. Building cairns with Wisdom, making this a path with no path, one worthy of following.

WE ARE THE ONES

We are unraveling
The sacred parchment
Singing out in languages
That we forgot we knew

We are decoding
The future's blueprint
Written in the space
Between me and you

We are the Ones
We've been waiting for
Ancestors behind us
And ancestors ahead

We are the longing
Of our children's children
Reaching back to pull us
Through the veil of time

We are the echo
Of every kindness
Freely given
Pass it forward
Between your heart and mine

We are the Ones
We've been waiting for
Ancestors behind us
And ancestors ahead

Sapling Grove

Your People

These are your people
the ones who
push
the ones who
pull

This is your honest stand
the one you
took
in the kitchen
today

This is your prize
the one that lies
deep
in the pain,
open

These are your people
the ones who
push
the ones who
pull

MARCHING ORDERS

It has taken 17 years
to move back home
to accept and be accepted by
the island that
made me my own
and to find the bones I buried
in the woods as a girl

A dollop of land, this finite place
everything is recycled, reused
nothing goes to waste
even karma so thick
it's hard to wade through
growing tangled deep
forest of my heart

Rewriting the places that
were soaked in memories
I dodge the familiar forms
in the produce aisle next to me
trying to avoid
coming face to face
with my younger selves

A glass bowl held steady
the history of others in my hands
helping elders to cross
the street who helped me
to cross as a child
together we stand
links in this chain

Lopez called me back
a shrill whistle at recess
to return from the big world
clutching the elixir
of education, experience, heartbreak
back to the roots buried
back to the roots visible

Back to the heartwood
names of my childhood
stack of time's bedrock
building thick sentiment
 "When am I?" is the question
waking up different
always in the same place

The workshop of coming home
is path daily chosen
I take my marching orders
from a nursery of tiny raccoons
in a tall bent snag
as they peak their masked faces
from their hollow to listen
I sing to them for hours

Rejoining this waving island tribe
has taken everything I have
and given everything I need
trading anonymous for the fishbowl,
the blank page for the written story,
trading all other mountains
for this single one

New American Dream

Cast off!
we keen on the coming tide
clip keel and cut and glide
windward with change quick at our backs
down the rising glass sea

Ahoy!
Blue green swells, white sails bloom
rough of plank but tight and smooth
yar she is and sleek of bow
dug from the Mayflower's grave

Sails unfurl!
bowsprit points forward and steady
pressed in our Sunday best and ready
canvas snaps with rope so heavy
we slice into this new way

Westward ho!
Bless this voyage white-capped and clear
Scouring the bright line for Hope to appear
Palms facing far horizon we pray
Out to the wide wide sea

REPORT CARD

My child is getting A's
in everything except collaboration
buried knee deep in our shame
we are failing in this
most important subject
of working together

We circle the biggest lie
of separation daily
in the squirming space between
mowing the lawn and praising the wild
fickle and pickled,
we twist in the wind

There is no one-way liberation
just a drunken bumbling
that slowly became the American Dream
over millennia of Ponzi schemes
here we are, still sleeping

The stakes have to be stacked
pie sky high to
persuade ourselves to trade
our plastic trophies of independence
for the unsung power of unity
so we keep piling

Meanwhile, Nature patiently waits
with four billion years of straight A's
growing to die, dying to grow
offering her wisdom
of something worth
waking up for

EACH BEAD

On the endless necklace of now
many beads are threaded
each one shaped and colored
in the oven of
my own mind
my own heart
my own hand

Some so fine, first touch, cherry wine
some so heavy, so cold, cut
by the sharp gravel
of sorrow
a rusted ingot
scraped slow
scraped low

But most moments, like this one
a mix of warm and cool reflecting
dancing ourselves alive
a tiny disco ball
scattering joy
mirroring facets
mirroring faces
this bead, a beautiful mess,
early on Christmas morning

LET IT IN

It's your turn
to open a gift

All this stubborn love
that is trying to be shared
may be clumsily wrapped,
ungainly taped, and
awkwardly tied
with all the shiny
and distracting loops
of best intentions

It's your turn,
all eyes on you

Set down the phone,
the blame, the story
of who you have been
up until now, now
set down the wooden spoon,
and all the lovely distractions
of your hard won
and precious role

It's your turn,
let it in

Take the present
into your open hands
hold it, feel back
to where this love
came from, now
let the way you receive
be what changes things
for good

THE ONE WHO WASN'T

We don't talk about them:
the ones we didn't have/ the ones we couldn't keep.

I don't talk about him:
the one I still named/ but never sang to sleep.

But, we don't doubt the choice we made:
for all the years
of freedom gained
but pay full price
in conscience stained
for the ones we couldn't keep

We find them in our shadowed dreams:
the ones we didn't birth/ the ones we didn't know.

I sing a prayerful lullaby:
for the bright spark who offered/ I had to let him go.

Still, I wonder who he'd have become:
a man, a father,
a precious son
whose adoration
would be second to none,
instead of a faded shadow.

We don't cry about them:
the ones we had laid down/ without obituary.

I can't forget about him:
the one I denied/ yet couldn't bury.

And every year in late September,
I stand with the dark sea
to remember
his absence
in the shape of surrender
engraved on the locket I carry.

I Bring the Dawn

For Nonie

Early for carpool
perched on cold leather
pale blue world
we wait silent together

In the skylight above
shown mirrored below
a hundred droplets of us
all set to go

As a 6th grade twin
and dressed to match
your friends, not me
right down to the hats

This background music
songs that you've chosen
show where we've been
but not where you're going

One day, in less time
than we've already shared
you'll exit my world
with your strong shoulders squared

My eyes sting from this rising
of preemptive sadness
instead of savoring
a proud moment of gladness

Not wanting to hijack
I turn swiftly away
from this rare moment
at the crack of the day

My sweet sunshine girl,
we must keep pressing on,
but oh, how will I breathe
when you bring your own dawn?

TIGER CHILD

For Jax

Tiger Child, you came one arm bent
shielding yourself, a warrior emerging
your skin changing colors, face morphing
until you landed on this, your current form

Tiger Child, when I asked for 'teacher'
I did not expect you, fervent with passion
not in this armor, leading with "NO!"
fierce as a cornered bear

Tiger Child, conjure a vision of hope,
harness yourself to the
chariot of righteousness, sharpening
vulnerability as your best tool
no need to push, no need to hold back

Tiger Child, wield your power
with grace and mercy
channel your rage against injustice
in ways that create health, not harm

Tiger Child, when you are wounded
may you have a true friend
and the wisdom to receive
deep healing found only through love

Tiger Child, your battlefield is strewn
with the tiniest watercolor wildflowers
soft enough for you to lay amongst,
to dream into, sighing

Tiger Child, you have the impossible job
of fighting with an open heart
and I, the impossible job
of mothering a warrior

Tiger Child, no one is more loyal
than when you lead the charge
spear forged of pointed wisdom
with eyes as deep as Earth

GIFT OF BIRTH

Birthdays are a time to touch
rounded stones that *click click*
against each other
deep in the pocket
of my favorite green coat

Soft silk buttercream
lining rips slowly
as you both tumble
towards the light of day
one falling towards life
one falling away

and I, in the middle, standing still

daughter, carrying you
for nine months
so close there was no telling
was I in you? were you in me?
then in one perfectly natural
alien moment I met you
emerging from me
—chain of life producing itself—
a pain and a joy beyond all others

to be the spark
that lights up
your gray eyes
to be the gentle voice
in your head
urging you to try
to be the heart
that meets your darkest sorrow
is my brightest joy
as a mother

and I, in the middle, standing still

mother, being carried by you
for 49 years plus nine months
so close our spirits balk
at the task of separation ahead
I have always been the warmth
to wrap your drifting life around
allowing you to set anchor
to stay safe and hold
even as the storm of age sets in

to be the spark
that lights up
your gray eyes

to be the gentle voice
in your head
urging you to try
to be the heart
that meets your darkest sorrow
is my brightest joy
as a daughter

and I, in the middle, standing still

Birthdays are a time to touch
rounded stones that click click
against each other
deep in the pocket
of my favorite green coat

Those who love more win
but I will also lose
you both by Life's design
as you each step into the full light
of a bright new day
one towards life,
and one away

Mother Tree

MOTHER TREE

Calm and weary tree lean down
Cover me in fragrant gold
To melt like chocolate rain in bark
Like sheep into the fold

Of sinner's heart and wooden flesh
I warmly tangle in it
I marry bones and blood to dirt
And am complete this minute

There is a union sitting here
Of roots and toes and soil
Nature's hearty goulash stirred
And slowly comes to boil

Of lover's heart and wooden flesh
I sweetly tangle in it
I marry heart and mind to Earth
And am complete this minute

Please cedar tent of boughs embrace
My pale and chilly form
I finger needles, a pokey lace
And am at once, reborn

MOTHERS' RELENT

Once you cross over
the thick line
called 'motherhood',
there's no turning back
for while the needs
of your children change,
they never, ever end
and just as you get used to things,
they begin to shift again

When the time comes
to step out of my sight
child of my flesh,
my heart takes flight
and a part of me, but older
flies beside you
off your left shoulder

That fluttering of feathers?
those are my wing beats
the compulsive and nurturing
bower of sweet
swooping and looping arcs
widened by the year

carving curved patterns
of love in the air

You can't shake me
no matter what alley you slip
no matter what
tunnel pins you
in shadowed grip
my spirit will find yours
as yours found mine
the night your spark caught
and brightened with wine

May this part of me,
the best part, I pray,
fly with you always
(not of my own will,
for I am tired and
long for the stillness
of perch on shaded
windowsill)

But decreed instead by
a relentlessness growing

the joyful pain
of a deeper knowing
what in every language is
an unveiling, an uncovering
of life's essential role,
known simply,
as mothering

My Mother, My Soil

My mother once said
a parent's job is to accept their children
and a child's job is to invite the parent in

She read the poems of the Earth to me
held me when I fell, called me back
when I could hear no other voice

When I emerged from her
she taught me how to stand
to see the world's canvas, brightly

"I" first existed as an urge
a spark in her mind
a distant persistent call

She was my soil, built from her flesh
my bones grown from hers
my blood mixed from hers

This job I have requires no work
only the risk of transparency, like a glass door
opening from the inside, to welcome her in

UNBROKEN

My mother stands on her undug grave
green is the grass, yellow are the buds
"Right here." She points down.
I have no response.

She's taking care of me still,
under this blue sky, preparing a future
that she won't know.
this is how she loves.

She passes me the heavy basket
slow motion, red tablecloth
from childhood picnics
sitting side by side

Atop of this Earth, unbroken
we share Swiss cheese, her favorite,
orange carrots sticks, dark chocolate
and the view from above

I do not understand how,
but I know that I will be
"Right here." I promise her.
she has no response.

The Gemels:
embrace of fir and cedar

I Bring the Dawn II
for Clive

Bring me dawn in your
coarse hands cupping
my face tilted upwards

Bring me dawn in warm darkness
when my animal self burrows
into your nook, safe

Bring me dawn
inside of our joke
slyly shaking head
eye corners sparkling
(no one else needs to know)

Bring me dawn
from behind
muscled arms
buckling me in
for the briefest pause
of breath

Stopping together
this kitchen, our church
to touch the world that exists only
between our beating hearts

COMPLIMENTARY OPPOSITES

Inside the lead cauldron of this year
boils an alchemy of grief and gratitude
a simmering of liquid lace
frothed with gold
and rimmed with grace

Without hurry or hesitation
lie down with me here in the dark
here is the refuge born
by absorbing
the dense of night

As the dragon's tail
sweeps across the deserts of regret
be still and know
we have arrived
at the center point
of the great turning

Without hurry or hesitation
close your eyes with me
thick lashes, soft cheeks
and dare to reimagine "success"
not as achievement
but as a forest cathedral

The stained glass of leaves
sunlit music on the layered floor
all connected, all protected
directed by life's conductor,
a symphony of complementary opposites

Without hurry or hesitation
come drink the stars awhile
I have found a grassy divot
in the fragrant hillside
no one knows we are here

THRUMB

When I put my eager ear to your trunk, I can feel the thrumb
heartwood pulsing slow,
rooted far below
outwards, outwards
stretching down the hill.

Under the yellow napkins of farmland draped below
stitched with silken mycillium
your shoots grow
threads spreading, reaching
sewn under the shining ribbon of road.

Layered under the charmed cemetery
where my mother's thick white bones
will soon feed you
as she fed me
and knit us tighter, tighter.

Cheek on your damp bark, with whom do I share my roots?
Our fingers lace above our heads, bodies locked
rocking together,
resigned at last
to sweetly sink
thrumbing, thrumbing
far below the surface

THE RING

He accidentally threw
his wedding ring away
casually tossed it
tipped with a clang
into the yawning bin
without a thought
behind him

The next day he stood
wringing naked hands,
holding hopeful breath
preparing to dig, but
—it was already gone—
carried on final passage
over the wide gray sea
"Away" to where
the red dragon sleeps

This most sacred circlet
a scratched but glowing symbol
of our scratched but glowing marriage
lost to a foreign land
under useless mountains

of things/things/things that
we want, we buy, then scrap
plastic rotting refuse
and maybe the last resting place
to the most precious thing
we have yet to lose

HE

Sometimes when he looks into himself
into brief undisturbed brackish mirror
pooled in the thickest heart of wood
he glimpses all that he is carrying
the tallest rack, a crown of thorns
the tangled histories rough growing
prongs sprouting from the bloody
conquests, the pound of rutting:
the wilds of pain and pleasure
spurring prines without check
bursting out from itself
branching with age
with no concern
for weight,
for wield,
nor heft

Ribs heaving, barrel matted cords straining
rootbeer color, musky, ripe in otherness
he who knows these shrinking forests
bears this title heavily, staggering to
give completely, with a long moan
into forest floor, soft wet needles
nostrils sucking pink morning mist
bellow heard by the hushed birds

into crush of alder, weary bone
antlers juddering, prodding
under fallen dancing tree
lowering intricate burden
that he has carried
for so so long,
long enough
to be
done

HOLD TIGHT

I do not know what to do with my hands
I turn my senses to the Earth
feeling the pulse of springtime
under my bare and naked soles

Touch is the new currency
silky smooth and liquid
skin on skin, skin on bark
to caress this pink and plummy branch

I do not know what to do with my hands
I kiss the water's taut surface
I lick the dewdrops from slender new shoots
squeezing fistfuls of dirt until my palms hurt

Touch is not lost,
it is just underground
come into contact with this smooth
beach stone deep in my flannel coat

I do not know what to do with my hands
I am touching you right now with my words
let them in, the embrace that you are craving
Can you feel this?

Hidden Mirror Pond

Your Nest

A collection of twigs and feathers
memories and dreams

The place where you fit perfectly
made for you

By your hands, your heart
sheltered from storm

A promise awaits
the day of your hatching

What conditions, my love,
will ripen your cracking?

TURNING TOWARDS

Turning away from screens
and their shallow roots
a worn mother holds her
head in her hands

Seeking ease of refuge
deep in delicate bracken
of towhee and ravens' rook
lost in mottled shadows

In this wilder family
a mother can lift her face
to birds, and to the rain
to the love within the pain

While her heart courses
with felted human grief
she rejoices for the world
of so much more than that

BURNING TO HEAL

I thought when I burned
my first marriage down
the flames that engulfed
even the loyal Douglas Fir
would burn out just as quickly

(how wrong we are about pain, tho
how deeply misunderstood,
the spiral ways of wisdom)

Twenty years older
my bare soles still
catch upon glowing embers
steaming in the damp soil,
a searing surprise,
and burn again

Nothing hurts as much
as the flames we light ourselves
and nothing serves the landscape of spirit
like a gulping wildfire,
quenching its thirst with ash

(how wrong we are about pain, tho
how deeply misunderstood,
the spiral ways of wisdom)

It takes courage to strike the first match, yes
but even more to wander
through blackened ghost trees;
to accept the grim and valid
faith of destruction,
the daily choice of resurrection

Courage is searching
for tender vermillion shoots;
learning to love the
unrecognizable forests
that have grown up where
once there were only
vast and smoking fields

LET IT FLY

Let the desire to honor life
displace the fear of loss
a white bird that flies
from cupped hands
on the steps of this crumbling temple
let it fly, you will not miss
holding it captive

Trust your instincts to close this chapter,
to read the descent of an arc
let your last words be "thank you"
for true endings stick
when gratitude
is the only thing left
in your mouth

It takes courage to be done
to follow the exit signs
without drama or panic
to allow the natural cycle of endings
to be complete
and to firmly close
the door behind you

GRIEF AND GRATITUDE

Grief and Gratitude
are fierce lovers
they fuck and fight
until they lay spent
on the sticky upstairs bed
in angles so immodest
it makes them both
howl with laughter
until they cry

DIVINE EXHAUSTION

Tired behind my bones
long brittle branches
keeping everything up
bending
bowing
down

Tired behind my voice
sugar-coating long gone
straight-shooting for truth
aim
pull back
let fly

Tired behind my eyes
like a child searching late
on Easter morning
running
looking
running

Tired behind my ears
straining to hear voices
as they filter through the wind
animal
plant
spirit

Tired behind my heart
longing to return
beyond separation
towards
the
one

Tired enough to lay
my leaden head
in the lap of the divine
trusting
weeping
purring

THE PACTS WE MAKE

I made a pact with the Universe
to never be a single mother
watching my own, tall and freckled,
singing her stoic song
strains of lonely freedom
bending from all that weight
day after day, year after year
not my lot, I swore

I must've pledged early on
a furtive commitment,
voiced to the sweeping currents
only remembered
deep in the trying
as another negative red line appeared
facing myself down in the tiled mirror
I recalled holding a different wand
casting a younger spell
upon this older self

Oh, the power of a promise!
once remembered,
how quickly we tied that knot!
the fastest bowline thrown
eloping in a borrowed apricot dress

a size too small, in a different town
away from comparing eyes
and familiar altars, one witness
instead of three hundred to pledge
 "I do", "I am", and "I will"
delighted to wear the shroud of wife
as fair payment for motherhood

Oh, the power of a promise!
a week later the hostess of the Universe
smiling at a promise kept, ushered you,
a patiently waiting seed guest,
to your readied womb
making comfortable for nine moons
to grow inside the most grateful and
rotund hotel in all the land

SABOTEUR PARK

My Achiever yells, "GO!"

My Avoider says, "NO."

My Drama Queen loves to steal the show

My Victim is hurt

My Bully throws dirt

My Martyr rips hundreds of holes in her shirt

My Tyrant screams, "MINE!"

My Cynic says, "FINE."

My Rebel breaks in and steals your wine

My Pleaser nods, "YES..."

My Controller hates mess

My Perpetrator shames you and makes you undress

My Whiner just whines

My Bad Girl does lines

My Conniving One gets out of paying her fines

My Restless can't BE

My Greed cannot see

My Scared Little Girl just wants to flee

Oh, Me? Where is "Me?"

Hmmm........Let me see.....

A WITNESS TO HEAVEN

Ashes of roses fall
from Zeus' careless hand
turning the ocean to wine
falling, the sky is falling

I'm tipsy from this
shameless layered display
the cosmos is showing
her petticoats to me

Shy as any voyeur
I pause at the guardrail
unsure of my role
in the making of such love

SMASH

"Caution: contents flammable"
should label every human
as the tindered grass of pride threatens
to ignite the dreaded deadwood
of collective trauma, personal drama

The humbler's skill
of telling on the self
is a critical and tangy ingredient
in the recipe for sanity
in the recipe for truth, for wholeness

Pace yourselves, friends
after skinning the slippery ego
comes the longer, harder work
of casting the family china
a thousand times to the marble floor

Let compassion bend you slowly
towards the child
who crouches amongst the shards
of what used to be such
a pretty and intricate heirloom pattern

HOME OF BELONGING

I am building a home of belonging
from repurposed intention
mossy grey pounded shoreline
tall black sway forests
of fir, damp cedar, alder

I belong to the roaring walls
of solstice fires
the ritual yearly witness of
our island children as they cross
the threshold, flower crowned and grown

I belong to the Salish sea,
the teacher of patience as I learn how
to wait for boats
and wait for boats
and wait

I belong to the awe of the tides,
ocean of emotion
twice changing in a day
a reminder of how much
is in constant shift under the surface
in and out and through
the narrow ripping straights
pulling between the craggy channels

I belong to the slicing barnacles,
tight black-lipped mussels,
bright sandpaper sea stars,
each one a party favor for the soul

I belong to deep teal kelp alleyways,
woven with sleek shots of seals
gunning for sockeye
breaking the tension
with loud whelps! of air
to gaze with detachment
towards our land-lubbing ways

I belong to the people that came
before us in the crunch of
clam shells underfoot
joyful reverence, smoke of salmon
sacred in longhouses
sweet scent of hand hewed cedar
singing to the same spirits
that I sang to in the forest
this morning, repurposing intention

I belong to the story
of the Orca whale, Mama Tahlequah,
nosing the sucking currents,

pushing her stillborn calf
around our shale island
for seventeen days without eating,
consumed by grief,
tireless, as if to say,
"See what I have loved and lost.
Do not look away. See this. Feel this."

Just like her,
I belong to what I love
when we love something
with our whole heart,
we belong to it forever

Grotto: rustle of sword ferns

RISE

Women of the Earth rise
up from the quiet landscape
swell of mountain, secret of valley
to know and be known
by that tree, that vine,
that flitting bird just off the hardened path
singing "Theeee! Theeee! Theee!"

Women of the Earth rise
beginning with skin
taking back the face,
name, breasts used to
please, placate, and pretzel
not by swift revenge, but with calm dedication
because it is the women's work of the day

Women of the Earth rise
and bow to nature's laws:
interdependence, regeneration, collaboration
laying down wide planks of story
fitting mine next to yours
and hers and hers, to become a living bridge
to walk across with raised eyes and sure feet

Women of the Earth rise
holding the spark of creation within
never to be extinguished
our fuel bright with blood
we bleed and bleed but do not die
we are the Holy Grail
never owned, and never dry

Women of the Earth rise,
right action flows from
prayer inspired by nature
filling the whole world
with holy manuscript
drawing all hearts closer to
Thee! Thee! Thee!

SING TO ME OF SILVER

There you are
your comings and goings
for thirty-six years
of lunar embrace
as a large glowing pendulum
pulling sharp on my blood

Show me now
your even-handed
cool reflection
soft and distant
sending those watching into a silence
louder and finer than singing

There you are
it is you I feel
obscured, then bright
coming and going
your generous inconstancy
lighting the path on the water ahead

Show me now
the skin I must wear
as my tide pulls out
and I, earthly woman
must continue this
mysterious shifting of shape

LISTEN HERE

To save a life by listening
requires two ears, one heart
and enough time
to hold the rope for another
as she dives deep
entering the silent
crush of pressure
cold color of darkness
holding still enough to bear
the courage of witness, to hear
her secrets that are true
her secrets that are lies

To save a life by listening
requires trusting,
in her own time
by her own power
she will know to follow the
line of her truest words
hand over hand over hand
pulling upwards towards the
shimmering bright above
breaking one day—maybe today—
the mirrored surface of
her pure and rippled self

LEY LINES

Ley lines of power
etched around my eyes
fanning creased curtains
round the windows of my soul
looking out from this body
I can see the freshness of youth
staring back, incredulous

I too remember thinking
that age would not touch me
that somehow I alone
might be spared
the challenge of
the lobster
growing beyond its shell

Defying mortality
costs us our life
a hobbling of spirit
to the tyranny of fear
lest we celebrate
time's gift wrapping

From these visible weather patterns
slowly emerges
a personal cartography
of genetics and will,
causes and conditions,
sun, laughter, worry
choices made, not made
so much sacred information
buried in the ley lines of a smile

BLAME IT ON EVE

In this orchard
all is ripe
hanging low and heavy
gravity pulling down
persistent with
passion

This apple wants
what every woman wants

To be savored
juices appreciated
her beauty inspiring movement
her wisdom planting seeds
deep enough to grow
better versions

This apple wants
what every woman wants

And when the fruit
can no longer resist
trading vantage for connection,
it must trust through surrender
let go fully, and fall
willingly, fall
to the ground

NOT OF GLASS

For your information
we aren't made of glass
light shining through
translucent, numinous
but no, not fragile
not breakable, not tenuous
women were never
two dimensional
we have always known
how to hold the bread knife
how to hold the baby
how to hold the world
the morning after it burns
so in a moment of forgetting
if you ever let fly
that stone dug from the
landslide of fear
that you hold
behind your back
and your rage is true and clear
and makes contact

we will not shatter
for we are not there
not made of glass
not to gaze up at while
sleepy in Mass
nor colored with stain
beveled nor buttered
not leaded, not brittle
nor easily shuttered
for your information
we can't be contained
gazing on high
from such beautiful pane

CAN'T TAKE IT WITH YOU

I saw the oldest woman in the world today
paper thin, angel duft hair
downy as a duckling
peering out a car window
looking into me with
the knowing eye of a whale

Oh, the journey she takes
from cradle to grave
promises made packed
into scuffed family luggage
dented and embossed
with someone else's initials

Ticket stubs and rocks to rub
photos of him, of her, of them
the book she wrote, a shy wooden boat
a red satin dress, small things of 'yes',
a gold locket with the letter "S"

The oldest woman in the world
neatly lines up three valises
bulging with memories
standing pretty in a row
right here, right here
by the worn stage door

DEATH OF A PLEASER

She'll beg as she kneels
she'll plead for her life
she'll promise you anything,
anything twice

She shows understanding
so raw and so true
brightening and lightening
the worst parts of you

Speaking your language,
she hits the bull's square
to the eye of your ego
with compelling flair

She feeds as she nurtures
seducing your stay
and pivots towards wooing,
a creature of prey

So, who will do the deed?
what executioner dares
to strike down the one
whose pleasure they share?

Will no one take the sword?
can no one see behind
this mask of appeasement
that leaves everyone blind?

(Of course it is an inside job,
as all deaths must become,
falling a thousand times
upon her whetted blade
before the job is done)

CIRCLING

Do not underestimate
The circle of women

The offered hand of a stranger
The quickness of sister

When there is no out but in
A soft voice reminds me

That I am my breath
To sit up, drink water

"You can do this"
Gently makes it so

Reminds me that
After this impossible push

Over the sharpest edge
There will be, Inshallah,

Resolution and maybe,
Blessed, blessed rest

THE WAVE

I had a vision of a wave last night
That is rising in the ocean
The water's black, but in the pale moon light
It is swelling and building with emotion

I will rise, she will rise
We will all rise together
And when this wave breaks
Upon a new dawn
Our lives will be changed for the better

I had a vision of a wave last night
That is building, building in the ocean
Moving fast now, in this silver light
The moon, she calls us into motion

And I will rise, she will rise
We will all rise together
And when this wave breaks
Upon a new dawn
Our world will be changed for the better

View From the Hammock
at the Top of the World

Box Canyon

I think I am alone

up parched arroyo
slanted stone lasagna
canyon pulls me
following the dark trickle
as a lover towards her source

I think I am alone

when through a throb of cicadas
and hot bitter sage
sure sweet notes soar
the kind of song
I sing when

I think I am alone

unfiltered honey, open throat
drips down cliffs
dark with petroglyphs
into my spying ears
my pace falters, stalls

I think I am alone

closing my eyes, protecting his
privacy, as his oval voice
crashes in communion
of sound, sand and stone
what human folly to ever

think I am alone

CREATIVITY IS A RIVER RUNNING

Creativity is a river running
rolling flowing coursing gunning
moving inside
never dry
touch it
touch it
lean out, try

Oh no, I can't, I might fall in!
what if I forget how to swim?
it's too fast
too much
too big to touch
what then?
what then?

Learn to trust the current that swells
let go of the bank
give in,
give in
rolling flowing coursing gunning
creativity is a river running
who knows where I will ride?

COURAGE FOR THE WIDEST LEAP

We do not know
what to think
but we know
what we are feeling.
Let's go with that

We are off the map
throw away the key
'shoulds' unraveling
faster than we can write.
Let's go with that

We lead with our hearts
like horses bred for dressage,
the only way to hurl
our proud hearts over the fence.
Let's go with that

ALL THAT POETRY IS

for Amanda Gorman

A bouquet of old words
arranged in new ways
emotion unbottled, to influence
another way of seeing, of being
leaders that we
ourselves would follow
turning phrases that
turn our minds
towards the divine
a voice filled with sunshine
parting leaden clouds
a sign of our times

This is all that poetry is

The writer must bow her pen
to that which breaks her
heart a little—or a lot—
depending on the courage of the day
the size of the audience,
the depth of the play
to follow the tears

they know the way
for within the heavy dismay
and shuttered longing for a new day
we may, with invitation,
climb on the back of these words

This is all that poetry is

Alight on these thoughts
of bright dragons we soar
down and through, up and over
to dismount, amazed
in lush landscape ungrazed
inside of fresh colors, new rules,
we stand serene, unfazed
a hidden treasure buried deep
in the reaching mountains
of our worn country
we stake claim on this

This is all that poetry is

29 FLOORS UP

for Mary Oliver

I walk this tight hotel room
naked, disbelieving
the hard news that has caught me
in the act of changing

She used to write while walking
feathers from the wind
spirals from the ocean
the whole round world, her kin

Arranging sacred prompts
on honeyed windowsills
saving us through beauty
just as saints are doing still

It was grace that moved her pen
writing as if blessed
nobody beats gravity, not even
she, who loved Earth best

TRANQUILITY AWAKENS

On the other side of the mountain of Fear, just beyond reach
of the cold shadow fingers, Tranquility is waking up.

It is still the heart of Winter. The white bones of the trees shiver
outside, standing still after a long night of dancing to the winds of the
Northeast- a storm that brought news of unrest and possibility, twisted
invisibly together.

Tranquility rises slowly like mist from her creamy nest of linen and
soft wool. Her long limbs draped in the ivory shawl that her mother
brought back from India for her, woven by ancient hands and embroi-
dered with tiniest prayers and tinier blossoms.

Her bare feet shiver in delight to meet the smooth wooden floorboards.
Cool as freshwater. She stands.

This is her home. Tranquility doesn't mind the company of others, as
long as they are good with not talking. But she is always her own best
company.

Her dwelling is elegant in its simplicity. Carved beams arc above her
like a tall upended boat. Flames catch bright in the stone hearth with
little effort.

She only owns one cup, one bowl and one spoon. The spoon is from
her great grandmother Josephine's silver set, and grows warm with
holding.

Outside of her window in the bluing light, the song of the forest begins.

The feathered ones begin to call, softly at first, then more boldly with the brightening, celebrating another dawn, another dawn. The birds are not scared. Even after that storm. They know in their hollow bones that without this reckoning, there would be no Spring.

Tranquility pours the tea. Turns towards the fire, and holds her cup with laced tapered fingers. The steam rises to explore her smooth features. She breathes in the scent of mint, oat straw and lemon-grass. She breathes out gratitude.

Tranquility knows that without the mountain of Fear behind her, her home would not exist.

She puts her hand to her chest. Closing her eyelids, she opens to the quiet temple within.

Tranquility bows to what she doesn't understand.

Soon enough, when she is pulled, she again will pack a simple bag and follow the brackened path that winds up into the dark.

But not yet.

ALLIES

Look to the rat
who has lined the nests
with news clippings and bits of soft flannel
ripped from our father's shirts
clever and sheltered
quietly content with these
incredible shrinking lives

Let us trade in our security
for freedom now
it is time
to pass the flask
and drink deep from the bottle
marked "Unmask"

Look to the bat
who dances above
in the darkest spaces
using the echo of truth
to wayfind
winging forward
full speed and blind

Let us trade our need of information
for the urgency of expression
we were made to shout and stamp and sing!
under all this great pressure
the weakest parts break first
floor boards buckle and crack underfoot

Look to the beaver
industrious and strong,
let's put our backs into
the great restructuring
clearing away stubbornness
to gnaw, slap, drag, rebuild,
never mind the downpour

Let us humbly ask
for fresh vision
holding hope over chaos
to trust ourselves at last
all hands building habitats
to redefine what it means
"to serve and protect"

Look to the phoenix
growing from these ashes
mystical made real
through sweat and courage
creativity rising
on feathers of pure flame

Let us press close
in this darkest night
praying to new allies,
and dreaming of first light,
when the hour will brighten
veins of purest virtue
to glow and grow from within

STILL POINT

I try to stay on the path
but the bluff calls too loudly,
the way she does
spangled with buttercups
waving her lilac flags

I follow the twig-legged deer
dixie-cup hooves
winding upwards over
crosswords of fallen trees
under bowers of Oceanspray

Cushions of bright moss
beckon me down, down
I enter the miniature world
the mossy forest below
tiny mysteries beyond naming

Clacking Madrona leaves
preen above arching
smooth backs swaying
branches touching, dancing
I join the Earth's breathing

Dark boughs gather
swaying together
murmuring, nattering, muttering
at the human form
curled and small below

And then, no wind
the forest talking
loudest in the silence
melts all but the longing
to stay nested here

But the dog beside me whines
and the stomach growls
and the fat raindrops begin to fall
and the outer world calls me
back to the path again

Boughs That Reach
But Cannot Touch

GONE GIRL, GONE

My precious once
and true friend,
I thought
we were in that
"For a Lifetime" category
So strange.

Death wouldn't
be easier, I know.
This slow fade
of an old favorite song
—so strange.

How can
we forget
the very things
that once made us
feel most alive?

At one time
you called forth
that best side of me,
the side I turned
towards the camera.

Now we are
just smiling
faces in a box
behind other boxes.
Estranged.

Out of touch,
no touch,
nothing touching
but this chime at the
stroke of memory
chanting,
'gone girl, gone'

Oh, did I mention that I miss you like chocolate?

FORGIVENESS, LIKE SALT

I carry the apology around
like a packet of salt
in my pocket
tight, heavy
moving it between coats

to fully accept your truth
to allow your anger
with a strong spine
a soft front,
a hand on my jilted
tenderized heart

It seems I require this
gentle rhythmic thumping
small salty weight
a reminder of
of what I long to learn

HELD

There's no better listener
than the forest
once good and lost
I sail my spirit into the sky roots
cradled by this hidden womb
damp with mosses

I ground down
between the spicy needles
through the thin layer of topsoil
the busy threads of fungi
into the cracked bedrock
and beyond familiar
into substances unknown

While so much falls away
nature grows in kindness
how could I fail to trust
this layered rhythm
a visual song
of secrets kept
and all things forgiven?

There's no better listener
than the forest
this place where all hatchets are buried
even that razor sharp one, that you swore
you would never let go of

even that one
even that one

Four Peas in a Pod

Sitting with my childhood sweetheart
in matching swivel rocking chairs
we are pointed in the same direction
to the party loft upstairs
where four teenagers
shriek with laughter

not the rocking chairs we thought we'd sit in

"The most karmic relationship I've ever seen."
said the astrologer and shook his head.
"So many layers …", we took the challenge
a month before we wed
knowing our path
would be a rocky one

everything happens for the best

Heavy is the burden for the one who remembers:
Bellingham, Berkeley, Bend, Santa Cruz, Pai, Y2K
other blurry New Year's Eves
so far far away,
I am the only elephant
in the room

memories cannot be willed or wished away

And even though we have to work
not to compare the lives we live in separate houses
not to finish each other's sentences,
nor to compare spouses
nor children
nor photo albums

still, there is a rightness to all of this awkward

Those of us in small towns are never far
from touchstones rubbed smooth,
from paths not taken, vows bent and broken
beyond anything left to prove,
my first true love,
our parting did forge

the two sets of siblings howling high above

AUTOMAGICALLY!

The morning after I dream you flying
you automagically rang at my door
holding a tall sweet
steaming black tea, milky
curling like a long cat's tongue
just when I did not know
I needed it most

I automagically look up
when the gold slants
through pillared silhouette
pointing my eyes toward sound
I remember your whispered voice
 "If you can hear the bird
 you can see the bird"

To spy the ruby crown
my heartmind thrills
long in body, a dark arrow
of Pileated Woodpecker,
a-rapp-tapp-tapping
Morse code of purposeful rhythm,
automagically!

OPENING

When we risk
our heavy Winter identity
the unseen doorway
of friendship
swings open smoothly

trust this

The generosity
of a pale pink blossom
shy and insistent
signals the beginning
of a more colorful season

hallelujah!

Answer the quiet knocking
of a new face, a new place
risking made easier
with the first pulse
of Spring
to open, at last,
into a fresh room
singing with light

Ghost Root

CHILDHOOD VIEWFINDER
SUMMERS AT THE RANCH

7:
through the diamond head
metal fence
I watch my father's bowed back
as he walks away
towards his bigger duty
to help the:
Hopi/ Navajo/Apache/Zuni/Vietnam Veteran
(Fill in the blank underdog)
meanwhile we are
locked in a kennel
day care prison camp

10:
granny's thin cornflower dress
pulled from the mothball steamer trunk
my horse waits, long neck bowed
watches me strain
to latch the loop of wire gate
fingers cramp
dog pants
powdered dust of ponderosa pine
hot tin water from the dented scout canteen

my rebellion is a quiet escape
beyond calling distance of log cabins
up the jeep road to Bosco
freedom is this alone
rattlesnake fear
playing the edge of safety

14:
from the stovetop
hot rock tip top
I hang my clothes
and rough towel stubble
on butterscotch
willow bending
my last year naked
awkward entry
can't get in fast enough
the dark of my beloved oiled creek
shying from assessing eyes
my flesh melts liquid
visible only to myself under the surface
water, my first lover,
dissolving my own harsh judge
with caresses that awaken

17:
a casual promise
overly given
by The Father
loses meaning
and begins to eat away
at other
bigger truths
I harden to the distinction
between good intentions
and follow-through
deflating paternal integrity
like a birthday balloon lost under the sofa
revealed only by its lack

21:
someone please tell me
what is the point
of all this Mensa education
when you sell the
bones of Great Grandfather
and Great Grandmother
and the corn-fed dreams
of the son and daughter
to the highest bidder?

SECOND BORN, SECOND BEST

My father is a flock of dark birds
Momentarily blocking the sun

My father is the smell of pipe tobacco,
Yardley soap, boot polish, old dust

My father is an Amtrak train-rider
Boundary-crosser, monologuer

My father is his beloved books
Multiple copies, each more significant

My father is the Strawberry moon
Rising over the meadow of nostalgia

My father is the tangled labyrinth
Of people, places, dates, overlapping

My father is the pure love of a dog
Crooning, gentle stroking of upraised head

My father is the paying of all dues
"White man on the Rez", exiled

My father is a silent gargoyle
In cold stillness crouching next to me

My father is a rough stolen hotel towel,
Rolled around a warm Coors beer

My father is the perfect arc of a jackknife over
The darkened water of the creek

My father is an old stack of Playboys
Carton of Camel cigarettes, rings of cheap coffee

My father is a devout Quaker
With a dark snake of jealousy nestled in his heart

My father is the low bass of the family band
Raised in raucous harmony

My father is gingerly stepping over
The hot metal cattle guard

My father is blue Hopi cornmeal
Rubbed into an old wound

My father is the heavy cream
Swirling into steaming liquid black

My father is nibbling on burnt toast
On chocolate, on a chicken bone

My father is the polished oboe, long-neck banjo,
The 28 autoharps stacked in his attic

My father is a pair of Levis slipping down
Pregnant with toxicity, with unborn potential

My father is the sweat-stained Stetson
Princeton stripe, the sandcast bolo

My father is the book that never got written
The degree never submitted, the road trip untaken

My father weeps at the Vietnam memorial
Tracing with guilt the lives he could not save

My father carries the victim's torch
But has no one to pass it onto

My father is the grudge, never forgiven
A grace that's never fully been given

A Prayer to Hermes on the Day of My Father's Burial

The father finally leaves
as she knew he would
the heavy door clicks
she is alone, feeling
white and dark indigo,
relief and sadness

Relief like singing alone
in an empty room
sadness as sudden
as this departure
a lost wedding band
a father's gentle hand

These dark and hazy hues
of sadness and relief
wind around each other
like snakes around a staff
Hermes, trickster messenger,
escort him intact

Cut free of form
deliver the father's bones
bent under the weight
of the mother's fear
down to the place
where color has no name

These same bones
carried her on high
down to the creek
tall upon the shoulders
through the barbed wire
over slicking rocks

She sings a prayer
medicine of harmony
her small voice rising
—Can you hear me, Dad?—
through the thinnest veil
of this empty room

MORTALITY'S PROBLEM

Just off stage we hear its wings
it keeps us up at night
a bony feathered trapped poor thing
box nailed shut and tight

The problem with mortality
are the chains we braid from fear
hell-bent dreamers stuck in motion
a compulsive shared nightmare

We mow, and mow and mow the lawn!
blowing the leaves around
little piles of rust and dust
upon decaying ground

Thoughts of something bigger brighter
make our minds' jaw snap
we've forgotten that we're timeless
no dot upon a map

Best to scuttle, dodge and dis
this promise of certain end
but instead who might we become
to take Death as a friend?

Dying's become our common villain
assassin of our roaming
the last note played by an oboe reed
high in the gloaming

Once given honor she will rise
and set our lives a'wing,
Death, our one true birthright
—that poor and twisted thing—

WHEN WE GO

Hope will fly like a pair of swans
lifting as one from the marsh

When we go

The poems we live
are the ballads to sing
words fired loud
by scattershot wing,
swans rising up
as queens and as kings
forgetting their reasons for pride

When we go

Out of the Woods, Under the Sky

RETURNING

All of this drama!
from the swell
of hopeful heartbeats
to the crush of despair
breaking darkly
drawing downward, pulled
without compassion or care
by the living Ocean body

Every sigh of pleasure
every sob of anguish
every gasp of insight
every yawn of release
every increasing scream
pulled up and out
by the insistent pulse,
gravity of growth,
more demanding than
any known machine

We, the raindrops,
have no choice,
adding our part

with courage of
surging surrender
to cleanse and feed
the voracious Water Cycle

As the Ocean is pleased
by ancient snowpack
our traumas, exclamations, exhalations
splinters and chunks of frozen time
are welcomed by surge and spray
frothing displacement,
with majesty and thunder ,
before melting, slowly,
back into its own

FIRE SEASON

Roots curling backwards
I stand so very small
in the face of this
roiling beauty
hot naked face
tipped skyward
empty hands held up
searching for blue
and begging for rain

I am not naive enough
to believe these tears
could ever
put out a flame
my despair, it seems,
is part of the
scorched landscape
horizon punch line

All that is left
is to bow, astonished
by the courage
of Earth for washing

herself clean in a
surging sea of fire, wondering
from a place beyond time,
what will rise someday
to dance among this ash?

PRAYER OF BREATH

Wings open and shut
breathed every second
by tissue pink butterflies
rhythmic and true

For rich and for poor
in soft treasured chests
these bellows of life
play the same measured tune

now smoke chokes our byways
we struggle for breath
the pulse of our planet
beats out of time

To expire or inspire?
the global heart spasms
it will take all we have
just to follow the signs

Each inhale, a "Please"
each exhale, a "Thank you"
a gift freely given
to the old and the young

The yearly tempo
of 6 quadrillion
breaths taken
this unnoticed blessing
of prayer from our lungs

PERFECT STRANGER

the courage to beg
is a line uncrossed
an empty bowl
thin arms,
head bowed
asking a silent, "Please."

to watch as shame
turns her back
rejected, in his
hour of need
digs a sudden chasm
of fear on both sides

giving a gift
without audience
speaks of devotion,
bringing a stranger
closer than kin
by the swiftness of love

humility asks us
to split our hearts,
the ripest peach,
free from its skin

to share the juice
of abundance with the world

those who see
beyond "other"
pour goodness
to overflow the ditches
along side the dusty road

THE DREAM THAT DREAMS ME

We are thousands marching slowly, coming from every direction. Over crumbling rock bridges, past impossible spires, we walk in lines towards the place, the one place, the sacred canyon.

In a desert with two moons, orange sand, licorice sky, we are draped in rough pale cloth.

We march for a long time- days? months? There are more of us coming from all directions than I can ever count.

Sometimes there are children...

I recognize familiars from my dreams before, greeting one another with slight nods. We carry light in our cupped hands, moving inwards towards the place, the one place, the sacred canyon.

I smell hidden grottos, stardust, cold ground. Looming cliffs surround, softly streaked with forgotten water. The color of earliest dawn stretches pale above.

The round nullah is perfectly silent, save for the grainy swish under our naked feet. So many flames held in so many cupped palms. So many feet, walking towards the place, the one place, the sacred canyon.

In wide arcs we place our tiny fires to burn together, even the children, making opening circles of light. We face the middle and pray this way.

Everything is sacred if we pilgrimage towards it.

Everything is sacred if we carry it in our hands.

Everything is sacred if we place it on the altar.

CONTRARY

Contrary to what your minds says, you are not alone,

not an island, whose ice -precious- is melting.

Contrary to what your mind says, your hands are not empty but held solidly on either side by those who came before and who will follow after.

Contrary to what your mind says, you belong right where you stand, part of this unbroken line, a colorful key sentence buried in the long story.

Contrary to what your mind says, your single thread of this great fabric is not unraveling, but dancing free in the salty wind.

Contrary to what your mind says, you are not falling apart, but falling back together.

Contrary to what your mind says, nothing is more important when you step out of your car carrying too many gravid grocery bags than to sit on the frozen gravel driveway, lean your head back and look up and out —Oh the dazzling splendorous night! —before going in.

TASTE OF SUMMER

Jewels dull and ripening
blackberry hanging low
so juicy and sodden
insistent in its fullness
deep in the barbed wayside

I did get a few, though
when I remembered
to go slow to go fast
discerning ripeness
by feel, tug and slip

I finally made it out
with a classic plastic jug
tied with milky yarn
cutting into my shoulder
"One for the bucket, one for me..."

Don't you sometimes
get that feeling in early Fall
like you couldn't spend
enough gleaning time
harvesting it all?

GOLDEN

And now
all I have here
is this thin slice of time
the ripple of licorice clouds drifting in
and a patient four-legged friend in the back field
can you smell winter in the soil, too?
every stalk will soon fall
yes, of course we will
but this slanted light
this moment,
so right

Cairns on the Path

Down Into Owl Valley: When we walk in nature, we are formed by nature. Receiving this wisdom through adventure takes time, determination, and receptivity. As we embark on the path that we have walked many times before, we give ourselves permission to explore the mystery of the familiar.

The Sapling Grove: New things are growing. The young lean into what light and space that is available, growing up from the crumbling stumps of the past. In witnessing and nurturing youth, we celebrate life's persistence; feeling the frustration, anxiety and compassion for the increasing challenges these saplings face to thrive where they are rooted.

Mother Tree: The mother tree is the most nurturing and grounding essence of life. It is central, deeply holding and deeply held. This is where all things are traced back, the origin of our roots.

The Gemlings: Is it one tree or two? Merging at its base, the gemling is a living story of two conjoined trees that fused together, self-grafting. In all true partnerships, collaboration must prevail over competition. The roots that grow beneath the gemling must ultimately form a stable base so that both can reach and grow.

Hidden Mirror Pond: We all have secret, quiet places where we go to reflect on our own growth. In the privacy of our thoughts, we glimpse visions of who we have been, who we are now, and the possibility of who we are becoming. These places of tranquility give clarity, but can also distort our seeing.

The Grotto: Rustle of Sword Ferns: There is a power of many things rising together. In certain conditions, there is a surge of growth. In the shelter of each other, many move together as one in the wind, waving their points and making a noise that is both soft and deafening.

The View from the Hammock at the Top of the World: When we arrive at the summit, there is a chance to sit and take in the view, The top of the climb is a place to absorb celebration, to catch one's breath, and to experience contentment and inspiration.

Boughs that Reach but Cannot Touch: Sometimes those growing close together are unable to connect. They lean towards each other, longing to meet. No matter how much effort or intention they have to form a union, they remain separated.

Ghost Root: Things have to be upended in order to see their true power. When shown the underbelly and extent of decay of the fallen, there is an appreciation for the complexity of life and questions of life and the questions of death.

Out of the Woods, Under the Sky: Coming back is a process of integration. There is relief, soreness, and the gratitude of return. Insights and expansion want for weaving into the comforting cloth of home. Time to rest.

ACKNOWLEDGMENTS

I would like to acknowledge the support of my husband and soul-partner, Clive, without whose championing of my creative spirit, this book would not be possible.

I honor my mother, Asha Lela, who has modeled love of the land since her days pioneering as a single mother when I was a small child. I thank her for her constancy and for showing me what Home means.

Our children give me great purpose to use my voice. Thanks to Nonie for her positivity and to Jax for the ways in which his fierce love calls me forth.

My brother, Chris, has always been an example of living into one's purpose. Thank you for that inspiration.

My childhood friend, Faith VanDePutte, offered the title, *Walk Deep*, and is my constant soul-sister. Thanks to Carolyn McGown for her skillful and sensitive copy-editing. I want to also thank Heather Mitchell for her brilliant structural ideas and sunny friendship. I appreciate the bright light of dear friend Britney Westervelt and am grateful to Regna Frank-Jones for the longevity of our loving connection.

I'm grateful to several writers who have supported me on this journey: Iris Graville for her mentorship and for her encouragement to enter the Homebound Poetry Prize contest; Kip Greenthal for her grace and dedication to literary expression; writing teacher and author Lisa Jones for inspiring me to write from the senses; and the surprising friendship of best selling author Manda Scott whose unique combination of writing and leadership has been influential in this work.

I want to acknowledge the communities of learning that have held me during this project: The Viral Poetry community who generously received my raw poems with unflagging encouragement; The Co-Active Training Institute that gave me such a solid foundation and skills with which to build a life of meaning and fulfillment; The Spiral Leadership community and my dear friend and colleague Sarah Wildeman; Pir Shabda Kahn and the Ruhaniat Sufi community; the Easy Writers; and the wider Lopez community for raising me up and continuing to shape me.

I give thanks for my delightful canine companion, Bella. Her steady adventuring presence is a balm to my soul.

Finally, I bow in deepest gratitude to the beautiful, wild Earth, and specifically the lush island of Lopez who continues to nurture and bedazzle. I give thanks to the Coast Salish people who have called this island home and have cared for her from time immemorial.

ABOUT THE AUTHOR

Abigail Morgan Prout has worked as a Co-Active leadership coach for the last 23 years, helping thousands of clients to hone their leadership presence and impact. For 8 years Abigail has served as faculty for the Co-Active Training Institute, leading their coaching and leadership courses. She is passionate about poetry and creative imagination as a way to cultivating leadership. Abigail returned to the small island of Lopez with her husband Clive to Washington State to raise their two children, Iona and Jax. She can be found rambling, singing, and listening in the coastal forest every morning with her silky black lab, Bella. *Walk Deep,* her first book, won the 2021 Homebound Publications Poetry Prize.

WWW.ABIGAILPROUT.COM

HOMEBOUND
PUBLICATIONS

Since 2011 We are an award-winning independent publisher striving to ensure that the mainstream is not the only stream. More than a company, we are a community of writers and readers exploring the larger questions we face as a global village. It is our intention to preserve contemplative storytelling. We publish full-length introspective works of creative non-fiction, literary fiction, and poetry.

Look for Our Imprints Little Bound Books, Owl House Books,
The Wayfarer Magazine, Wayfarer Books & Navigator Graphics

WWW.HOMEBOUNDPUBLICATIONS.COM